Bean liked to catch insects and flies. He was good at jumping up high and catching a fly. He was good at grabbing spiders.

One day Jelly and Bean were in the wood. They came to a crooked tree. Bean saw a crack in the crooked tree's trunk. He looked inside it.

He saw lots of bees. One bee flew out of the crooked tree trunk. "I will catch the next one," said Bean to himself. He stood by the tree and he waited.

A big bee flew out of the crooked tree trunk. Bean jumped up. He tried to grab it. "Ow, ow, meow, meow," he cried.

The bee stung Bean's front foot. "Meow," he cried. He shook his foot, but the bee was stuck to it. Its sting was stuck in Bean's foot.

Jelly came to help Bean. She looked at the bee stuck in his foot. She made Bean stay still. The bee pulled itself free. It flew away.

There was a little hole in Bean's foot.

There was a little spot of blood on it.

"Oh, I'm bleeding," cried Bean. "Look at the blood on my foot."

Then his foot began to swell up. "Oh, look at my foot," cried Bean. Then his foot began to hurt. "Oh, my foot," cried Bean. "I have a pain in my foot."

So Bean limped out of the wood with Jelly. He limped all the way back to the little shed on three feet. He lay down on the hay and he went to sleep.

The next day Bean's foot was not swollen. The spot of blood had gone. Bean felt better. He was catching spiders now. They did not sting.

"oo"	"u"
good	jumping
wood	up
crooked	trunk
looked	stung
stood	stuck
foot	pulled
shook	
blood	(front)
look	